Explore
Scottish History

STUART SCOTLAND

RICHARD DARGIE

Explore Scottish History is packed with historical evidence  to help you discover how Scotland's people lived in the past. It also includes links to the Heinemann Explore website and CD-ROM ⊙.

Heinemann
LIBRARY

www.heinemann.co.uk/library
Visit our website to find out more information about Heinemann Library books.

To order:
☎ Phone 44 (0) 1865 888066
🖹 Send a fax to 44 (0) 1865 314091
💻 Visit the Heinemann Library Bookshop at www.heinemann.co.uk/library to browse our catalogue and order online.

First published in Great Britain by Heinemann Library, Halley Court, Jordan Hill, Oxford OX2 8EJ, a division of Reed Educational and Professional Publishing Ltd. Heinemann is a registered trademark of Reed Educational & Professional Publishing Ltd.

OXFORD MELBOURNE AUCKLAND JOHANNESBURG BLANTYRE
GABORONE IBADAN PORTSMOUTH (NH) USA CHICAGO

Designed by Celia Floyd
Originated by Dot Gradations
Printed by Wing King Tong in Hong Kong

06 05 04 03 02
10 9 8 7 6 5 4 3 2 1
ISBN 0 431 14524 5 (hardback)

06 05 04 03 02
10 9 8 7 6 5 4 3 2 1
ISBN 0 431 14525 3 (paperback)

British Library Cataloguing in Publication Data

Dargie, Richard
   Stuart Scotland. – (Explore Scottish history)
   1. Scotland – History – Stuarts, to the Union, 1371–1707 – Juvenile literature
   I. Title
   941.1'06

Acknowledgements

The Publishers would like to thank the following for permission to reproduce photographs:

Bridgeman Art Library pp6, 8 (London library), 13 (Scottish National Portrait Gallery), 15 (Scottish National Portrait Gallery), Corbis p24, Heritage Image Partnership (The British Library) p11, Hulton Getty p9, Mary Evans Picture Library pp19, 21, National Museums of Scotland pp7, 20, 23, Scotland in Focus pp5 (R Schofield), 10 (M Moar), 12 (R Schofield), 17 (R Schofield), 18, 22, 26 (D Burrows), 27 (D Barnes), 29 (Bob Lawson), SCRAN pp14 (National Trust for Scotland), 16 (Edinburgh City Libraries), 25 (Edinburgh City Libraries), Topham Picturepoint p28.

Cover photograph reproduced with permission of Bridgeman Art Library.

Our thanks to Ian Hall of the University of St Andrews for his comments during the writing of this book.

Every effort has been made to contact copyright holders of any material reproduced in this book. Any omissions will be rectified in subsequent printings if notice is given to the Publisher.

Any words appearing in the text in bold, **like this**, are explained in the glossary.

Contents

The House of Stewart

The Stewards or Stewarts were originally knights from northern France who became one of the most successful royal families in Europe. When the son of Robert the Bruce, King David II, died in 1371, he was childless. The Scottish crown passed to Robert the Steward. His family became monarchs of Scotland and England, ruling for almost 350 years.

The Stewart family ruled Scotland at a time of great change. Around AD 1400 the Middle Ages were coming to an end. There was a rebirth of interest in science and the arts. Distant parts of the world were discovered by explorers. Historians call this period of change the **Renaissance**.

The Stewart family turned Scotland into a stronger, wealthier kingdom. Scottish ships traded across northern Europe, and its people became better educated. Under the Stewarts, Scotland became a more peaceful country as all of the king's subjects were made to obey the law.

James I knew he had to control the local lords who raided and plundered the countryside. His first Parliament passed strict laws against nobles who raised their own private armies. James summoned the Highland chiefs to a Parliament at Inverness, then ordered their arrest. Three were hanged to show that the king's law must be obeyed.

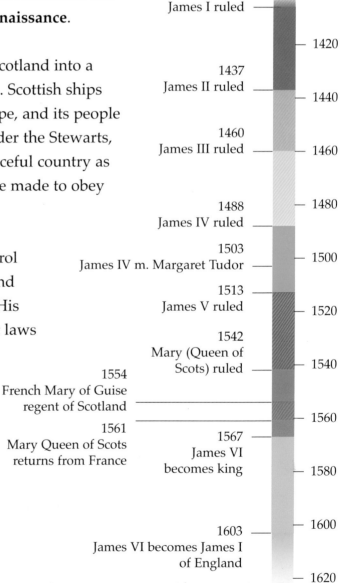

1406
James I ruled

— 1400

— 1420

1437
James II ruled

— 1440

1460
James III ruled

— 1460

1488
James IV ruled

— 1480

1503
James IV m. Margaret Tudor

— 1500

1513
James V ruled

— 1520

1542
Mary (Queen of Scots) ruled

1554
French Mary of Guise
regent of Scotland

— 1540

— 1560

1561
Mary Queen of Scots
returns from France

1567
James VI
becomes king

— 1580

1603
James VI becomes James I
of England

— 1600

— 1620

The Stewart Royal Coat of Arms.
The spelling of 'Stewart' was altered to 'Stuart' in the 17th century, during the reign of Mary Queen of Scots. It is said that the Scottish spelling of the royal name Stewart was changed to look more like the French pronunciation of the time.

The next Stewart king, James II, wanted Scotland to be strong in war. His Parliament passed laws to make sure that every able-bodied man was ready to fight for the king. Men aged between 16 and 60 years were ordered to practice archery.

James II was interested in the new science of **gunnery**. He brought giant cannon over from Europe. One of them, Mons Meg, can still be seen at Edinburgh Castle. Unfortunately, James was killed by one of his own guns called The Lion. It exploded during a siege at Roxburgh Castle in 1460 killing the king instantly.

James III worked hard to unite his subjects under Stewart control. He chose the thistle as his country's emblem and stamped it on the coinage. The royal standard of the Lion Rampant was carved upon buildings throughout the kingdom. This made Scotland feel more confident as a nation.

Exploring further

The Heinemann Explore CD-ROM will give you information about Scotland and the world from 1450 to 1700. From the Contents screen you can click on the blue words to find out about Scotland and the wider world.

The Golden Age of James IV

James IV was a great prince of the **Renaissance**. During his reign, writers, musicians and architects were well rewarded for their work. He even encouraged Andrew Myllar to set up the first printing press in Scotland in 1507.

James IV King of Scots

 James IV described by a Spanish visitor to Scotland

"James is of noble stature and handsome. He speaks Latin, French, German, Flemish, Italian and Spanish as well as **Gaelic**. He is courageous... and carries out the law without respect to rich or poor."

James continued to improve the education of the Scots. In 1496 his Parliament ordered every landowner to send his sons to school to study reading, writing and the law. James wanted these boys to grow into men who could help him to run the country properly. He also founded Scotland's third university at King's College in Aberdeen in 1495.

James believed that Renaissance ideas could make his kingdom stronger, richer and safer. He encouraged men of science to come to his court at Stirling. One of these was John Damien, a mysterious Italian alchemist who thought he could turn lead into gold in his laboratory. Damien was fascinated by flight and even jumped from the battlements of Stirling Castle wearing man-made feathers.

 From an Act of the Scottish Parliament translated into English

"It is ordered that all barons send their sons at the age of 8 or 9 to a grammar school and that they stay there until they have an understanding of the law."

"The Great Michael was the strongest ship that ever sailed in England or France. Her oak walls were ten feet thick, so thick that no cannonball would go through her."

James wanted to build a strong fleet to protect the kingdom from attack but also for trade with Europe. He built nearly 30 ships, and the most powerful of these was the *Great Michael* launched in 1511. This was the biggest ship in Europe at this time. It weighed over 1000 tons, had a crew of 300 seamen, and carried 120 gunners and their cannon. Building the *Great Michael* used up all the forests in Fife.

In 1503 James married Margaret Tudor, the daughter of England's King Henry VII. He hoped that this royal marriage would help to keep the peace between the two countries. However, in 1513 the English attacked France and James had promised to help his French **ally** in war. The *Great Michael* and the rest of the Scottish fleet sailed to Ireland and attacked English forts there, before sailing to join up with the French navy. James gathered his troops on the Edinburgh **burgh muir** and marched south into England. The two sides met in battle at Flodden Edge where the Scots were defeated. Although most of the Scottish army survived to carry on the war, James IV was killed and the Golden Age was over.

Exploring further – The Renaissance

James IV was influenced by the new ideas of the Renaissance. Read about these ideas on the CD-ROM. Follow this path:
Exploring the Wider World > The Renaissance.

New ideas about religion

In the Middle Ages, everyone in Scotland belonged to one Church. This was the **Catholic** Church led by the Pope in Rome. Every parish in Scotland had its own Catholic church and priest. The Church also ran all of the schools, colleges and even hospitals. The medieval Church was very rich and powerful. Most of the books in Scotland were written by Catholic churchmen. People who disagreed with the Church were imprisoned, and sometimes even burned at the stake as **heretics**.

After 1500 more ordinary Scots were able to read for themselves. They began to read secret books smuggled into Scotland by ships from Holland and Germany. The writers of these books attacked the Church for its wealth. These writers were called **reformers** because they tried to reform, or change, the Church for the better.

Books like this stirred up hatred of the Catholic Church and turned many Scots and English to being Protestants.

The most famous reformer was a German Catholic priest called Martin Luther. He called for the Church to change its ways, and finally he set up his own Reformed Church in 1525. People who joined this new Church were soon known as **Protestants**.

Luther's ideas spread quickly to Scotland. The first Scottish Protestant was Patrick Hamilton, a young student who had been to Europe and read Luther's books. He spoke openly about the need to reform the Church in Scotland. He was arrested and burned as a heretic at St Andrews in 1528.

From an eyewitness account of Wishart's burning

"The fire was made ready. When Wishart was brought to the stake, he kneeled and prayed, and said 'This grim fire I fear not. My soul shall sup with the Saviour this night.' Then he was put upon the gibbet, and hanged, then burned to powder."

George Wishart, a teacher at Montrose Grammar School, also became a Protestant. He was burned at the stake in 1546 for daring to challenge the old Church. The leaders of the Catholic Church hoped that these executions would stamp out the new Protestant ideas in Scotland. This didn't work. Many Scots were impressed by the bravery of men who chose to die rather than give up their new faith. On May 29 1546, a band of sixteen men broke into St Andrews Castle and stabbed Cardinal Beaton to death. This marked the beginning of the Protestant **revolt** in Scotland.

The last words of Patrick Hamilton at the stake

"I am more happy that my body burn in this fire for keeping faith with Christ, than it burn in the fire of Hell for denying Him."

Exploring further – Martin Luther

Discover more about the man who started the Reformation on the CD-ROM.
Follow this path:
Biographies > Martin Luther.

A Protestant land

Scotland was a divided land in the 1550s. Many Scots were loyal to the old **Catholic** Church, and also wanted Scotland to stay friendly with its **ally** France. Catholic Scots supported their French ruler, Mary of Guise. She was governing the country as **Regent** because her daughter Mary Queen of Scots was still a child. However, many Scots secretly belonged to the new **Protestant** faith and looked to Protestant England for help. They hoped that English troops and money would help them get rid of Scotland's French Catholic government.

In 1558 Mary of Guise ordered the burning of Protestant prisoners. One of these was an 83-year-old priest called Walter Myln. The execution of a harmless old man shocked many people, and the Protestant lords and merchants began to arm their men with weapons and supplies.

In May 1559 a Protestant preacher called John Knox returned from Europe to his native Scotland. Knox was a fiery man and a passionate speaker. After one of his stirring sermons in Perth, a band of Protestants ran through the **burgh** smashing holy images and objects in Catholic churches. Protestants in other burghs across Scotland did the same, hoping to 'purify' their churches.

The **Reformation** in Scotland had begun. The following year an English fleet and army arrived to help the Protestants. The French Regent, Mary of Guise, died and her French troops sailed for home. In August 1560 a Parliament met in Edinburgh to decide the future of the Church in Scotland.

 John Knox was a fiery preacher and a clever leader who helped to turn the Scots into a Protestant nation.

This Reformation Parliament abolished the Catholic Mass and rejected the power of the Pope. The Parliament set up a new Reformed Kirk or Church of Scotland. Members elected their own minister. In the old Catholic Church, leaders such as Cardinals and Bishops had been all powerful. In the new Protestant Church, ordinary Scottish people could have much more say in running the Church's business. They could also sit on the local committee or **Kirk Session** which ran the local parish. Each year, the Church was to hold its own parliament or General Assembly in Edinburgh.

 Knox fearlessly argued his Protestant views in the presence of Queen Mary who was a devout Catholic.

"We desire that prayers be said in every parish kirk on Sunday in our own common tongue and not in the Latin of the priest."

From a Protestant letter to Mary of Guise

 Mary Queen of Scots' view of John Knox

"His sermons are too long but he is the most dangerous man in the whole of my realm of Scotland"

Exploring further – The Reformation

The ideas of the Reformation swept across Europe. To find out about the English Reformation, follow this path on the CD-ROM:
Exploring the Wider World > Focus on: Tudor World > The Reformation and the end of the monasteries.

The young queen

On the morning of 19 August 1561 a stately galleon slipped into the port of Leith near Edinburgh. It was carrying a young woman of eighteen back to her homeland. She was Mary Queen of Scots, who had returned to her northern kingdom at a very difficult point in its history.

John Knox's view of Mary's return

"Mary's return brought no comfort to this country but only sorrow, sadness and darkness. The sun was not seen to shine two days before, or two days after, her return."

Mary had grown up in France. She had married the **Catholic** King of France but he died tragically young. Mary herself belonged to the old Church. However, she was planning to rule a land which had become **Protestant** only a year before and many Scots feared there would be trouble over religion again.

However Mary quickly announced that she would not interfere with the new Church of Scotland. Although she was a Catholic in her own private life, she was happy to let the Scots worship in their own way. She even threatened to execute anyone who attacked the Kirk.

In 1561 there was a riot outside Holyrood Palace when the people of Edinburgh learned that Mary had taken Catholic Mass in her private chapel.

In 1561 and 1562 Mary toured her kingdom, staying at the royal palaces of Falkland and Linlithgow. Everywhere crowds cheered their young queen who was tall, beautiful and intelligent. Mary spoke several languages and had a private library of over 300 books. She also proved herself a brave leader. In 1562 she led her own troops into the wild hills of north east Scotland in search of the rebel Earl of Huntly and his men.

From a letter written by an English spy in 1562

"The Queen of the Scots is tall of limb and fair. She has only to smile to turn all heads. She spends her time quietly and is much given to reading and conversation. Her careful ways have made her pleasing to most of her subjects."

By 1564, Mary was safe on her throne. However she knew that she had to marry and have an heir. Many Catholic princes in Europe offered to marry her but Mary knew this would anger her Protestant cousin, Elizabeth of England. Instead she chose Henry Darnley, a Scottish noble who had English royal blood in his veins. Mary and Henry married in the Royal Chapel at Holyrood in July 1565. As Catholic monarchs, they hoped to rule their Protestant kingdom in peace.

Exploring further – Queen Elizabeth

Throughout her life, Mary and her cousin Elizabeth I of England were fierce rivals. The Biographies section of the CD-ROM tells you about the lives of England's Tudor kings and queens, including Elizabeth.

The fall of the queen

In 1565, Mary looked safe on her throne. She had won over most of her Scots subjects and defeated her rebel enemies. She was happily married to Lord Darnley, and in June 1566 she gave birth to a son who would become King of Scotland and England. However, within only two years, she had lost her kingdom and fled into exile in England.

Lord Darnley

Darnley turned out to be a bully and a **fop**. Although he was called King Henry of Scotland, he was king only in name. He wanted real power but Mary would not give it to him.

Mary's downfall began soon after her marriage to Darnley. He resented the influence that Mary's friend and secretary David Riccio had at the Holyrood court. In March 1566 a band of armed men entered the Queen's chambers, and stabbed Riccio to death. Mary believed they were sent by Darnley, and had little more to do with him afterwards.

The following year Darnley fell seriously ill with **smallpox**. At Mary's request, he was lodged in a small house at Kirk o'Field near Edinburgh. On 9 February the house was blown up by gunpowder, and Darnley was killed. Many people thought that Mary had planned his death in revenge for the killing of Riccio.

Mary married for the third time, and this time her husband was the Earl of Bothwell. He had already been accused of blowing up his rival Darnley. The people now turned against Mary. They were shocked that she could marry her husband's suspected killer only three months after his horrible death.

A record of the marriage of Mary & Bothwell

"Upon the fifteenth day of May 1567, Mary by the Grace of God Queen of Scots was married to James Earl Bothwell in the palace of Holyroodhouse. At this marriage there were none of the pleasures or pastimes which are usual when princes are married......"

Mary lost the support of the powerful **Protestant** nobles. They forced her to give up her throne and imprisoned her in Loch Leven Castle near Kinross. Although Mary escaped, her few remaining troops were defeated at Langside outside Glasgow. Mary fled to England, hoping that her cousin Queen Elizabeth of England would help her.

Mary spent the next nineteen years in English castles. She was really a prisoner, and never met Elizabeth who feared Mary as a rival. Finally, Mary was accused and found guilty of plotting to take over the English throne. In February 1587, she was beheaded at Fotheringay Castle.

The death of Mary by an eyewitness

"Mary took off her robe and as she knelt down she repeated the 70th Psalm. Then she laid her head upon the block saying 'Into your hands Lord, I commend my soul.' One of the executioners held down her hands and the other cut off her head with two strokes...."

Exploring further – Portraits of a queen

The Digging Deeper section of the CD-ROM takes a detailed look at the life of Mary: Digging Deeper > Mary Queen of Scots
Click on the different topic headings to find out more.

In the High Street of Edinburgh

By 1600, Edinburgh and the nearby port of Leith were the biggest and richest **burghs** in Scotland. Edinburgh's High Street ran down from the castle, past the High Kirk of St Giles and the **Mercat Cross**, to the city gate at the Netherbow Port. From there, the winding Canongate led to the royal palace of Holyrood. On either side of the High Street, there were dozens of narrow lanes or closes.

Edinburgh was built along the narrow ridge of a hill. As it was a very crowded burgh, there was little space and buildings rose up steeply. Many were **tenements** or houses of six or seven storeys, divided up into flats. The first burgh houses were often built of wood but stone became more common after 1600. Gladstone's Land is a stone tenement that still survives today.

Rich and poor lived together in the tenements. Important nobles and wealthy merchants lived in the large-roomed apartments on the first and second floors. Poorer folk lived in the small attic flats. The cheapest rooms were down in the basement. They were damp and sometimes flooded when it rained. Edinburgh High Street was often wet and muddy, so womenfolk wore wooden stilts called pattens to keep their shoes dry.

Merchants and craftsmen sold their goods from booths on the ground floor of their houses. Edinburgh was full of expensive goods from Europe such as tapestries from France, silks from Italy and musical instruments made in Germany.

This drawing from 1647 shows how Edinburgh's houses were clustered around the High Street. You can make out the **tolbooth** in the middle of the High Street.

 As it was the capital city, the Mercat Cross of Edinburgh was ornate and topped by the Unicorn, the heraldic symbol of Scotland.

Some citizens of Edinburgh sold their skills on the High Street. The burgh's surgeons and barbers waited near the Mercat Cross for their customers. Chemists known as **apothecaries** made up medicines using herbs and spices. There were even travelling salesmen, called mountebanks, who sold homemade potions that could cure aches and pains.

As the capital of Scotland, Edinburgh life was filled with colour, noise and ceremony. Great nobles rode through the town with their followers on the way to their town houses. The King's carriage trundled through the streets to his palace at Holyrood, or to the castle in times of danger.

 A French visitor describes Edinburgh in 1600

"Edinburgh is a mile long and half a mile wide. Its great street stretches from one end of the town to the other and is both wide and straight as well as of great length. Its buildings are by no means luxurious however, for many are built of wood."

"The streets and closes of Edinburgh are narrow. The houses are so near that there is hardly any room for fresh air and this is harmful....."

A comment by an Edinburgh citizen, 1650

Exploring further – Looking at cities

Try comparing what you know about Edinburgh with other cities of the time. You can read about London in the seventeenth century on the CD-ROM.
Follow this path: Digging Deeper > Great Plague and fire: London in Crisis.

17

Life in a Highland clan

In Stuart times, most people in the Highlands lived in clans or tribes. Clan was the old **Gaelic** word for family. Everyone in a clan believed that they had the same ancestors and they usually shared the same clan name such as Grant, Fraser, Macleod or MacGregor. Most clans lived together on their own territory.

Eilean Donan castle in Wester Ross was the clan fortress of the Mackenzies and the Macreas. It was blown up by English warships in 1719 but restored in the 1920s.

Every clansman was loyal to his clan chief. He had to fight for his chief in time of war and provide services on the land for him in peacetime. In return, the chief promised to protect his clansfolk from enemies and share out the food stores in times of famine.

Highland clans often fought each other in bitter feuds over land, cattle and honour. The hatred between the MacDonalds and the Campbells lasted for centuries. Every clan had its own songs and bagpipe tunes. These kept alive the stories of great deeds done by the clan.

In peacetime, most Highland families worked on their farms. Good land was scarce and most fields were small and often stoney. The Highlanders invented a special tool to open their land for sowing seed. This was the cas chrom or foot plough made of oak tipped with iron.

 Highland clansmen were hardy warriors. They could march long distances quickly over rough country. They slept in the open, wrapping themselves in their long tartan plaids.

Most clansfolk lived in simple houses with stone walls and thatched roofs. The furniture was simple, and the family cooked and ate around the peat fire in the middle of the floor.

Lowlanders were often afraid of the Highland clans. The fierce men of the hills spoke Gaelic rather than Scots, and wore tartan plaid rather than breeches. After the **Reformation**, many clans stayed loyal to the **Catholic** Church. This added to the fears of the strongly **Protestant** lowlanders.

 From a letter by an English General

"The Highlander is happy to march long distances over rough ground, sleeping on the grass and taking water from the stream. He carries a musket, a small shield or targe but his main weapon is his longsword which they call the claymore."

 ## Exploring further – Daily Life

The CD-ROM will tell you about daily life in other parts of Britain and the world. Follow this path: Exploring the Wider World > Tudor World
Click on the topic headings, for example Rich and Poor, to read about them.

Witch hunts and persecution

Over 1500 people in Stuart Scotland were burnt at the stake as witches. Around 2000 more were accused of witchcraft and horribly tortured. Most of these 'witches' were poor, elderly women or ordinary villagers or townsfolk. Sometimes they were known for their healing skills or for their knowledge of the herbs used in medicine. Some were burned just for being the children or partners of suspected witches. All were victims of the witch craze that spread across Europe between 1450 and 1700.

Witches were first executed in Scotland by burning in 1479. They were accused of **sorcery** and plotting against King James III. The Earl of Mar was said to have asked the witches to use their spells against his brother the king. James VI also believed that witches were in league with the Devil and plotting against him. He was fascinated by black magic, and even wrote a book in 1597 called *Demonology* describing the powers of witches.

The Elders on the local **Kirk Session** had the job of finding witches in each parish. Often they hired a **witchpricker**. He looked for the Devil's Mark on the accused, pricking them with long needles to see if they bled. Witchpricking died out after 1662 when it was exposed as a dangerous fraud.

 Spiked collars were placed around the necks of suspected witches. This was done to humiliate them and make them look different from the other townsfolk.

Many Kirk Sessions refused to physically torture accused witches. Instead they kept their victim awake for three or four days and nights without sleep. Desperate to be left alone, the accused said what their torturers wanted to hear. They said that they met the Devil, flew to their covens on broomsticks, and cursed their neighbours' sick animals or children.

After 1670, most educated people stopped believing in witches. Books and pamphlets poured scorn on the idea of witchcraft. Sir George Mackenzie, Scotland's leading judge in the 1670s and 1680s, tried to help prisoners accused of witchcraft and to make sure that they were found not guilty. However the last witch in Scotland was executed in Dornoch as late as 1727. The laws against witchcraft were only done away with in 1736.

"On Wednesday, five women were burned at the stake for witchcraft. All of them confessed to dancing with the Devil."

From the diary of an Edinburgh burgess in 1659

This picture of the 'North Berwick Witches' shows them causing shipwrecks by casting spells around a cauldron – just one of the things that 'witches' were accused of.

Exploring further – Education

As education improved, people believed less in witchcraft. New printing technology made knowledge available to more people. Discover more about printing on the CD-ROM:

Exploring Scotland > Discoveries, Inventions and Ideas > Printing.

Crime and punishment

The Baillies were important men in Scotland's **burghs**. It was their job to keep the peace and punish criminals. The Baillies had the power to judge cases and in larger burghs, like Edinburgh, they sat in special courts. In smaller towns, a Baillie just stood at his doorstep and listened to the complaints that people brought to him.

Baillies made sure that the burgh laws were strictly obeyed. They fined townsfolk who threw their slops into the public street or let their animals roam around the lanes. Most wrongdoers were fined. The money collected was used to pay the Baillie's wages.

Some wrongdoers were imprisoned in the cells inside the burgh **tolbooth** or tower. Prison sentences were usually short. The burgh council had to pay for the prisoners' food and drink and this was expensive. Instead, most criminals were humiliated in the **jougs** or the stocks for a few days. Prisoners in the jougs were fed by their families and this cost the burgh council nothing.

 Many tolbooths had a high bell tower such as this one at Culross in Fife. This was used to summon the burgh folk to important meetings or in times of trouble.

Punishments were often very brutal. People who lied or swore had to wear the branks, a metal mask with an iron spar that pressed down on the victim's tongue. This was often used on women, and was called 'the scold's bridle'. Thieves were usually stripped, whipped and banished. Female thieves in the countryside were sometimes drowned, as this was the cheapest way of punishing them.

The punishment of a woman at Elgin in 1658

"Janet Coutts is ordered to be held in the jougs and then banished from the burgh of Elgin with a paper tied on her head showing her fault which is swearing and lying."

Prisoners were often tortured to get them to admit to their crimes. The **peruinkis** or thumbscrews crushed the victim's fingerbones. These tortures were only abolished in 1708.

Some prisoners avoided torture and pain by agreeing to become slaves in Scotland's coal pits. Others were shipped to the West Indies to work in the sugar and tobacco fields. Few of these slaves ever regained their freedom.

Serious criminals were executed, although this was quite rare. Murderers were beheaded by the burgh axeman. The richest towns of Edinburgh and Aberdeen both had a 'Maiden'. This was a guillotine that dropped a sharp, heavy blade onto the victim's neck.

Although it looked fearsome, the Edinburgh Maiden only beheaded about 100 prisoners in its long history.

From Edinburgh's court records of 1650

"Edinburgh 23 January 1650. John Job sentenced to be whipped through the town on the back of a cart, for marrying two wives at the same time."

Exploring further – Rough justice

We know a lot about crime and punishment because everything that happened in court was written down. There are some examples of punishments on the CD-ROM. Follow this path:
Written sources > Hanged for theft or Execution of a murderer.

The Union of the Crowns 1603

In 1603 a rider from London galloped into the great courtyard at Holyrood Palace carrying a grave message. Elizabeth, the Queen of England, was dead. Elizabeth had never married and had no children. Her throne had therefore passed to her distant relative in Edinburgh. King James VI of Scotland was now King James I of England as well.

King James VI and I

James had become King of Scotland as an infant in 1567 when his mother Mary Queen of Scots gave up her throne. James had proved himself to be a skilful monarch. He had curbed the power of the nobles and brought peace to the religious problems of the day. James was popular and life was lively at his court.

James had a claim to the English throne through his father Henry Darnley, who was related to the ruling Tudor family. There were others with a claim, but the nobles and merchants in London supported James as their next king. James had experience of governing. After 50 years of Queen Mary and Queen Elizabeth, many English people were happy to have a king again. Above all, James was a strong **Protestant** who would defend the Protestant Church of England.

James set out for London, taking many of the Scottish courtiers with him. As he toured southwards, James was welcomed everywhere by his new English subjects. The friendliness and the wealth of the English impressed the king. They lavished gifts and honours upon him, and James soon began to forget about his poorer, more troublesome kingdom in the north.

James describing his journey from Scotland to England in 1603

"I am like a poor man wandering about for forty years in a wilderness and barren soil – and now arrived in a land of promise."

This Union of the Crowns was good for the Stuart royal family but bad for Scotland. James only returned once to Scotland in 1617. The next Stuart kings, Charles I and Charles II, spent almost all their time in England. They just looked on Scotland as a place to raise money and soldiers for their wars.

The city of Edinburgh was a much quieter place after 1603. The merchants and craftsmen who had supplied luxury goods to the Scottish court now struggled for business. Scotland's government and trade were neglected.

Skilled craftsmen like these outside Holyrood Palace lost their most important customers when the king and his courtiers moved to London in 1603.

Exploring further – Portraits of a king

Use the CD-ROM to discover more about what James was like. To see more portraits of the king and other well-known people from the time follow this path: Pictures > Key People and Events. Click on one of the pictures to make it bigger. A caption will tell you what the picture shows.

Scotland and Europe

In Stuart times, the land between England and Scotland was mostly wild moorland covered in bogs and boulders. There were no proper roads from Edinburgh to the south. It was easier for Scotland's merchants to send their goods by ship to Europe, rather than send them overland to England.

Before the **Reformation** in 1560, Scotland's main trade was with **Catholic** France. Scottish merchants had special trading rights at the French port of Brest. Thousands of gallons of French wine were brought into the Scottish port of Leith each year. The palaces at Holyrood and Falkland were built in a French style.

After 1560, Scottish merchants preferred to trade in **Protestant** Holland, and were frequent visitors to Dutch towns. Dutch style houses with crow stepped **gables** soon appeared in the small trading **burghs** along the Fife coast such as Crail and Culross.

Scottish ships carried basic goods to Europe such as timber, furs, wool and coal. They returned carrying luxury goods such as fine wines and silks, which fetched high prices in the burgh markets. Some merchants made a fortune from this trade.

 Houses like these in Fife were built in the style that Scottish merchants had seen in Dutch and Flemish towns such as Delft, Bruges, and Antwerp.

"The Scots carry to France linen, wool, skins of goats and of conies [rabbits] and kinds of fish taken from the Scottish Sea and afterwards smoked or dried and salted. And they carry back salt and wines from France."

From a traveller's diary of 1598

'Danzig' Willie Forbes built a fairytale castle at Craigievar from the profits he made in the Baltic fish trade.

Other Scots went to Europe as soldiers. Bands of Scottish troops sold their fighting skills to the highest bidder. Some fought for Catholic France, others for the Protestant princes of northern Europe. A Scottish brigade fought bravely for Sweden at the Battle of Breitenfeld deep inside Germany in 1631. Scottish generals were also in demand. Sir John Hepburn formed the oldest surviving regiment in the world, known today as the Royal Scots. He also became Marshal of the French Army.

Scottish scholars also travelled widely on the Continent. Some were Catholics who fled to the Scottish colleges in Rome, Paris and Madrid. They trained as priests and secretly returned to serve the Catholic parishes in the Highlands. Protestants usually studied at universities in Holland and Germany instead.

Exploring further – Exploration

This was a time of greater exploration outside Europe. To explore the Stuart kings' American colonies, follow this path:
Exploring the Wider World > Focus On: Britain 1600–1700 > American colonies.

The end of the Stuart Age

When James VI died in 1625, Scotland was at peace. The reign of his son Charles I was more troubled. Charles wanted to rule his kingdoms without the help of his Parliaments. He believed, as most monarchs at this time did, in the "Divine Right of Kingship". That is, that God had put him on his thrones and he could rule as he pleased. Charles also wanted the Scots' Kirk to be more like the Church of England, which was under his control.

Charles I became king in 1625. This is a picture of his coronation which did not take place until 1633. He only visited Scotland once more when he tried to stop the Covenanters going to war against him in 1641.

Many Scots saw Charles as a **tyrant**. They signed a National Covenant in 1638 promising to fight together to defend the Kirk. War broke out in 1639 between the **royalists**, or supporters of the king, and the **Covenanters**. Scotland was plunged into a long **civil war** with several bitter battles and a brutal sack in 1644, when royalist troops massacred the citizens of Aberdeen. Most Scots thought the years of war had finally ended when Charles was beheaded in London in 1649.

"We the nobles, gentlemen, citizens and ministers of Scotland swear to preserve the Reformed Church of Scotland and to defend all those who enter into this Covenant in the common cause of Religion, Freedom and the peace of the kingdom."

From the National Covenant of 1638

Tombstones like this kept alive the stories of how the Covenanters gave up their lives for their strong Protestant beliefs.

Religion was to lead to many other troubles in the years ahead. An English army under Oliver Cromwell invaded Scotland in 1650. Cromwell tried to force the Scots into an unwanted union with England. There was also more trouble between royalists and Covenanters throughout the reign of Charles II from 1660 to 1685.

In 1685 James VII & II came to the throne. He was a **Catholic** and therefore feared by **Protestants**. They planned a rebellion in 1688 and James had to flee for exile in France. His Protestant daughter Mary and her Dutch husband William of Orange took over as monarchs, but the Stuart Age was coming to an end.

With the king away in London, the Scottish Parliament in Edinburgh slowly began to grow in importance. It moved into a new Parliament house in 1640. Although the king's ministers ran much of the Parliament's business, merchants and small **lairds** began to have a say in the country's future.

The long years of trouble between 1640 and 1690 left Scotland weak and divided in many ways. However Scotland's trade, its population and its confidence continued to grow.

Exploring further – Searching the Stuarts

To find out more about the sixteenth and seventeenth centuries click on search on the top panel of the Contents page. Pick a word from the keywords on the next page and click on Enter. A list of pages on the CD-ROM that mention this word will appear. Click on the names of the pages to find out what they show.

Timeline

1371	Robert le Steward becomes the first Stuart king
1406–1437	Reign of James I
1412	Scotland's first university founded at St Andrews
1424	James I puts down the powerful nobles
1437–1460	Reign of James II
1460	James II killed in the seige of Roxburgh James III becomes king
1479	First witch hunts and burnings in Scotland
1488	James IV becomes king
1503	James IV marries Margaret Tudor of England
1511	Launching of the *Great Michael*
1513	James IV killed at the battle of Flodden Field
1525	Luther sets up his Reformed Church
1528	Patrick Hamilton burned at the stake as a **heretic**
1542	Mary, the future Queen of Scots, born
1546	George Wishart executed
1554	French Catholic, Mary of Guise, becomes **Regent** of Scotland
1559	John Knox preaches anti-Catholic sermons
1560	Mary of Guise dies
1561	Mary Queen of Scots returns to Scotland
1565	Mary marries Lord Darnley
1566	Birth of the future James VI and I
1585	James VI begins to rule Scotland with full power
1587	Mary Queen of Scots executed by order of Elizabeth I
1603	Death of Elizabeth I – James becomes King James I of England
1617	James makes his only return to Scotland

Glossary

ally friend or partner especially in wartime

apothecaries early chemists who made medical potions and mixtures

burgh town with a royal license to hold markets and fairs

burgh muir common land close to a town where everyone had the right to graze their animals

Catholic belonging to the Roman Catholic Church – the original Christian Church of Western Europe

civil war war in which both sides are from the same people or country

Covenanters Protestants who refused to obey the official Church set up by Charles I and Charles II

fop vain man who takes a great deal of pride in his appearance

gable upper part of the side of a traditional house

Gaelic original language of the people of northern and western Scotland

gunnery science of aiming and firing artillery guns such as cannon

heretics people accused of disobeying the official teachings of the Catholic Church

jougs iron handcuffs and neckchains to hold prisoners, fixed to the walls of the burgh tolbooth

Kirk Session group of local men who helped the parish minister run the church in each part of Scotland

Laird Scots word for a landowner or lord

Mercat Cross official sign to show merchants where they could buy and sell goods in a burgh

peruinkis iron vices that were tightened around prisoners' fingers, crushing the bones as a torture

Protestants members of the reformed church which split away from the Roman Catholic Church in the 16th and 17th centuries

Reformation setting up the reformed Protestant Church of Scotland in the 1560s

reformers leading Protestants who argued for a break away from the customs of the Catholic Church

Regent someone, usually a mother or uncle, who rules a country when the real monarch is too young to

Renaissance period of change, discovery and exploration that changed the world from 1450–1650

revolt rebellion against the king, government or official church

royalists supporters of the Stuart Kings in the religious wars 1640–1690

smallpox very common disease in the 17th century which often left the victim's face horribly disfigured

sorcery name for witchcraft – the making of spells and curses

tenements traditional multi-storey Scottish buildings usually found in the centre of the larger burghs

tolbooth burgh tower where criminals were imprisoned and the burgh charters were stored for safety

tyrant ruthless ruler who treats their subjects badly

witchpricker professional witchfinder who travelled around the country looking for witches

Index